Paintings That Look Like Things

poems and translations

Derek Updegraff

STEPHEN F. AUSTIN STATE UNIVERSITY PRESS

Stephen F. Austin State University Press
PO Box 13007, SFA Station
Nacogdoches, TX 75962
sfapress@sfasu.edu
936-468-1078

For information about special discounts for bulk purchases, please contact
Texas A&M University Press Consortium
tamupress.com
ISBN: 978-1-62288-222-9
Cover and book design by Sarah Johnson

for Elizabeth

CONTENTS

Paintings That Look Like Things

Setting

ACT I

A country road. A tree.
And it is Evening

Samuel Beckett, *Waiting for Godot*

A country road. A tree. And it is Evening—
six words beneath ACT I in my edition—
a yellowed page whose sparseness is deceiving.
The reader brings the landscape to fruition,
as Beckett had to when he jotted *mound,*
low mound to be exact,
when seating Estragon.

What gets filled in cannot detract
from *country road* or *tree* or *Evening.*
The latter is embodied by the leaden sky
outside my window. And the road? Loose gravel.
The tree? A muddle ripened for the fragrance
of the hospital bed, the bus stop,
or the front-row pew unraveling
in this yellowed absence.

I.

Paintings That Look Like Things

She stands before the mass, studies its shapes,
its strokes, its colors and its lack of colors—
"Look for absence," he once told her. But he
was younger then. And maybe now he'd tell
her something else to look for. She moves to the
placard. No title. Steps back to the center,
pulls out a notecard, cupping it in her hand,
then returning it briskly to her purse.
She mouths some phrase, her eyes fighting for sense,
turning from the canvas to the engaging
faces only now surfacing around her.

   His early paintings looked like things: still lifes
with fruit and bowls, pitchers and cups. Oh! and
the portraits. Such precision. "A God-given
talent," she'd tell her son. Oh how she longs
to see those gifts being used. Even to see
what he had called his Lucian-Freud phase.
She'd gladly take those portraits now, the figures
that seemed abstractions to her then. She'd hang
those, gladly even, gladly taking down
each early canvas, each painting of a thing
as a thing, the likenesses of things hung
on her livingroom walls, covering peels
in floral paper. She'd take down her dearest
ones in the kitchen, the ones going back
to grade school, if it would mean appendages,
all things discernible if not familiar.

   The other viewers shuffle toward his next one.
She stands a moment longer. Then she inches
toward the placard again. A price but still no title.
"Titles help," she whispers. She slips a hand

into her purse, pincering her card of phrases
jotted from phone calls, from his excited voice
explaining what he's doing. She'll let one hang
above her couch, get coached on what to say
before her friends sip tea in Christmas mugs,
get armed with explanations gifted to her,
his payment for her patronage, his easing
the mind of one who hates not knowing,
of one now readying herself to view
the next in line, the next of what is there
and what is not there and known not to be
there intentionally for one reason
or another. And see her now, lips moving
with the breath once from her and now his own,
his words sustaining her when she can't
comprehend the things that others seem to get.

A Bird of One Kind or Another

A bird of one kind or another chirps
outside while I'm inside. It's night, and I'm
unsure of the hour just as I'm unsure

of other things, so many things, whether
that jabbering's from a warbler or a babbler,
a starling or, perhaps, a sparrow.

I'm sitting idly in the lamplight glimmer,
the front room curtains opened just enough
to pane my figure for this outside chirper,

whose image I can't glimpse in this singed
hour, until her tone reveals her: a lemon
crowned babbler (I know her well), rose winged,

lilac footed, like a pigeon, except
that she's a babbler not a cooer, babbling
in muted covers, pear colored and pear shaped

leaves with the right light on them, but grayed now,
outside, where pear is gray, lemon gray, rose
gray, lilac gray. Hollow musing, hallowed

babbler, outlast me, please. Outlast this worry.
Inside, don't let this brightness fool you, you
whose rest is measured out between each whirling.

On This Loss

He dreams about his funeral while sitting
in May's classes, projecting on each wall
his classmates filing into pews, her gritting
the teeth he loved, her sobbing for leaving, all
joining in, sobbing, friends and teachers, those
who almost cared enough about him,
her lip's quiver emptied because she knows
this is her fault, this life without him.

He'd pictured some things right when the day came,
but he misdreamed the one who'd shoulder
his absence. Another's grip consoled her
when he died, and she knew she wasn't to blame.
The seasons piled. His memory grew strange,
but still his brother weeps what he can't change.

What I Would Have Said to Mike Standing on the Edge of the Coronado Bridge

for B. C.

Get down from there and hear me out.
It's difficult for you these days.
I don't doubt that, and I don't doubt
you want your pain to go away.

It's difficult for you these days
because you're drenched in agony.
You want your pain to go away,
and most of it will fade, you'll see.

Because you're drenched in agony,
you'll towel it off with others' help
and most of it will fade. You'll see
all burdens ease the more they're held.

You'll towel it off. With others' help
allow yourself some time to know
all burdens ease the more they're held.
That, you have barely seen. Don't go.

Allow yourself some time to know
there's much to live for in this world
that you have barely seen. Don't go.
You'll soon forget about the girl.

There's much to live for in this world.
I don't doubt that, and I don't doubt
you'll soon forget about the girl.
Get down from there and hear me out.

Sonnet at Midnight or So, at an Arco Station in Long Beach

Two girls walked up and asked him for a ride
just as he'd finished filling up.
        He smiled and said, "I'm sorry."
        The two were newly styled.
"We'll pay," one said, revealing from her side
a ziplock bag weighed down with change. "We've tried
some cabs, but they won't take it." Her face was mild
and young but also seasoned. The other dialed
her phone again and stayed preoccupied.
        Not liking their alternatives, he said, "All right,"
and dropped them off at their motel, insisting that
they keep their bag of change.
        He wished he'd thought of something else instead:
to drain that tank and ditch their clientele, to race
across the night without exchange.

Tattoo Selection

for D. G.

"Have you decided what you want?" Dan asked.
His London-heavy Danish accent stepped
across the din of rowdy gypsies massed
inside Bar Islington. His question kept
its sense despite the rising threats that swept
away most other sounds. "Not yet," I said.
"I like the thought of Japanese instead

of something more traditional, but I'm
not sure." He took a sip, then said, "Well I've
done loads of both you know," and asked, "You're time
is ending when, next week?" I'd met Dan five
months earlier, back when I'd first arrived
to study English lit. He treated me
much like a younger brother; he'd buy my tea

and beers, and when we'd go out to a show,
we'd skip the block-long queue and cover fee
because there'd be a bouncer he would know
whom he tattooed. With regularity
I'd help him clean and close the shop; then we
would grab a drink across the street. "Just four
more days," I said. The gypsies by the door

had gone outside to settle a dispute.
We stayed, arms on the bar, a mess of ink
contourless in dim light. Always astute,
the barkeep heard our empty glasses clink
and poured the two of us a second drink.
"It's up to you," Dan said. "Once you decide,
we'll do it one night after hours." I tried

to think of anything I'd wanted to
get done, some cherished object that would stand
for some great meaning, but those were few,
and any such my puerile drives had planned
were long done by another artist's hand.
His shop had been my library, the space
in which I'd read Orwell and Ballard, the place

where I'd composed my final essay on
the longing of Clarissa Dalloway,
all while skilled portraits and designs were drawn
in skin with instruments whose interplay
of buzzes bounced about the room all day,
repeating and reworking images
that every client thinks is hers or his

alone: bulldogs and eagles once again,
more dragons and red koi. "What's one tattoo
that you have never done?" I asked. But then
I phrased it differently. "What would you do
if you could have the choice? . . . whatever you
desired." He looked up meditatively,
the pub grew quieter, and I could see

the bouncers having folks drink up their booze,
the houselights brightening, the glow that caught
the amber glasses left on tables. Those cues
did not apply to Dan and thus did not
apply to me, and so we held our spot
as doors were locked. "I wish I could tattoo
a pigeon," he replied. The image grew

concretely in my mind: Trafalgar Square,
the cluttered tourists trying to evade
the greedy packs of pigeons everywhere.

"A pigeon, Dan?"

        "They've got this vivid shade
of purple at the neck, their wings are frayed,
and some have spots of turquoise interlaced;
some even have clubfeet from acid placed

on windowsills. They're interesting, you know."
He took a sip. "So that's what I would do."
"All right," I said.

      "All right to what?"

           "I'll go
ahead and get a pigeon done." I flew
from Heathrow to the States days later, passed through
the customs line not claiming I possessed
a tattered London pigeon on my chest.

Friday Night, Years Back, Closing the Tattoo Shop outside King's Cross Station, London

We'd cleaned and locked the shop by 12:00 a.m.
He'd talked about his son throughout the day
              and how the two of them
would spend these coming weekend hours at play.

Each time his son gets dropped off by his ex,
he asks his dad to draw a green and black
              tyrannosaurus rex
across his chest, and SpongeBob on his back.

That image stuck more than most other ones:
the bright thick markers gliding on young skin,
              an imitative son's
desire to have his body colored in.

It stuck with me more than the lines of coke
he snorted in the late-night hours to come,
              more than a hardnosed bloke
walked home that daybreak by his straitlaced chum.

Early Lunch at La Valencia

Prospect Street, La Jolla

He tightened up his boots at 4 a.m.
By 5 he'd started work at his new site,
        where damp and gritty light
      encased him and the other men.
The coastal side of this hotel on Prospect
        had long been winter wrecked,
      but they would build it up again,
dismantling structures into separate piles,
removing junk while salvaging old tiles.

He worked on walls left standing by machines
whose clumsiness serves only to demolish.
        The tiles once they'd been polished
      up would guard the sleeping greens
and blues of summer waters. He loosened each
        within the careful reach
      of sledge and chisel breaking seams—
his arms outstretched, accustomed to the sting
of staying parallel between each swing.

He'd stripped down to a long-sleeve shirt by 8.
At 9 he and the others broke for lunch,
        assembled in a bunch
      and seated on discarded slate.
He'd seen most of these men at other sites,
        shared bread atop the heights
      of scaffolding. They'd congregate
whenever breaks allowed stilled hands to stifle
the work that feeds and clothes and builds this cycle.

This time he ate while watching waves below,
oblivious to conversations stirred
                at hand, for he observed
        the patterns formed by swells in tow,
how each crest crumbled at the very spot
                that broke the one it sought,
        where dark unmoving patches showed
him crowds of rocks beneath the water's face,
the hidden causers of that breaking place.

A wave builds to its peak, then shatters right
when it has crossed a depth half its own height;
                the place of impact switches when
                        the tide rolls in or out
or when the rocks and sandbars shift about.
                He'll work this job weeks more, and then
                        he'll work some other site,
a different scene first met in gritty light,
a different spot to break for lunch again.

My Unbelief Is Weeping in a Field

My unbelief is weeping in a field,
   crying for me to cradle him
   how I used to. At least a limb
to cling to, a body to be concealed

in, he's urging. My unbelief can't move
   from where I've placed him, always tilting
   toward me, his thin face wilting
while I'm blooming, in this light, in love.

II.

Between Pit Stops at Late-night Diners

Be wise, remove the dregs from the wine, and with the
space of our lives being short, prune away long hope.

Horace, *Odes* 1.11

Sweetness,
        You're right. Our route looks vague, but I
will always long for scrambled eggs and toast
at 2:00 a.m. with you, for the dark roast
of diner coffee with loose dregs, the sigh
of harnessed furniture, the fickle sky,
and for sharp winds colliding with the coast,
but I will long to keep long hope the most;
its limbs get pruned enough by passersby.

Let's let ours thrive among these grounds suppressed
by U-Haul traces and uncertain jobs
and pack it with us if we find it's time
to move again. Let's douse it with the best
of cheap champagnes, then marvel as it bobs
among treetops, magnificent, sublime.

                We'll keep it in its prime
always, our sweet long hope. We'll shovel it free
the second worry piles on its debris.

           Now in uncertainty,
let's keep each of our shorter hopes at hand
but not neglect the long ones we have planned.

The Third Season

Across the living room's worn floorboards, he
watches his wife design her first ballet
to Vivaldi's "Concerto No. 3."
The coffee table's pushed out of the way,
safekeeping her topped goblet of merlot,
while she is weaving movements for the show.

He's writing at their new garage-sale desk.
She's hearing strings of Autumn cause the sway
of leaves swept by the wind in arabesque
to *pas de chat* and tossed to *grandejeté*.
She jots the combination on a page,
then tests the steps on an imagined stage.

The melody begins with violins
and cellos backed by strings that alternate
the tranquil breezes with more violent winds.
Then lively pitches swiftly resonate
from flutes that bounce amid the steady sounds,
like leaves that rustle in their endless rounds.

She'd told him that her younger girls would play
the leaves while those on pointe portrayed the wind:
soft reds and yellow-browns in full array,
all jostled by the better disciplined
and older girls in delicate attire,
the girls reflecting her once-held desire.

He'd never had the chances to applaud
when she was Clara, Snow Queen, or Dew Drop,
Blue Bird, or Dark Angel in *Serenade*,
or give her roses by the lit backdrop,

and she has said she's grateful that they met
once she'd abandoned each false face and set.

He now observes the beauty and the grace
with which she moves, the ease with which she lifts
a leg and keeps her body's line in place,
fluidity of motion as she shifts
from foot to foot and effortlessly spins
in imitation of the restless winds.

Five months from now he'll see her students dance
Four Seasons. Then he'll watch his striking wife
ascend the stage once Winter leaves, advance
the floor that builds and breaks so much dear life,
then gently bow for her devised ballet,
his chance to offer his delayed bouquet.

The Things We Live Without

Do you remember how that charming place
where we first lived could barely heat the water?
You'd fill your baths halfway, and in the space
above I'd pour potfuls of what was hotter.
You'd bring your knees to meet your chest, and I
would carefully drop in what I had boiled,
trip after trip until you were neck high
in warmth and puffs of rising steam uncoiled.
Between the trips I'd sit as you caressed
my hands and newly filled-up pots began to bubble,
and then I'd stand and you'd say I should rest,
denying you deserved this little trouble.
These days our water always comes out hot,
but there are times I wish that it would not.

Ballet Class with a Blind Student Named Cricket

Her voice among the aisles
Incites the timid prayer
Of the minutest cricket,
The most unworthy flower.

Emily Dickinson

"The world has never felt so pure before,"
you tell the girls who leap into the air.
When little Cricket leaps across the floor,

the other girls are careful to be sure
to give her space, although she's unaware;
the world has never felt so pure before.

Because her blindness hinders her no more
than Ludwig's ears did him, the students stare
when little Cricket leaps across the floor.

She trusts your voice and hand amid the corps
of hopeful dancers swaying here and there;
the world has never felt so pure before.

Her mother waits just past the corridor
and sees the mirrors and walls completely bare.
When little Cricket leaps across the floor,

she sees a sea of eyes and hears the roar
of crowds who've come for her from everywhere.
The world has never felt so pure before
when little Cricket leaps across the floor.

Our Unmet Stages

She sleeps there on the couch, exhausted from
a morning of demi- and grande-pliés,
exhausted from her students overcome
with dreams to dance in their most-loved ballets.

She grips a pillow as her legs begin
to twitch. She thinks about her many girls
whose dreams will have to bend or break within
the coming years, as each harsh fact uncurls.

Life's sweetest days are spent embracing stages
that were never built for us to use,
when passions weren't funneled into wages,
when talents didn't guide the routes we'd choose.

There is no tenderness in skill's selection;
praise God there is in those who ease rejection.

A Warm Welcome to the City

Catullus 43

Hello. Good afternoon, young girl, whose nose
is hardly small, whose foot is great in length,
whose eyes are brightly dull, whose fingers, those
cherry-topped stumps, are poorly masked, whose strength

is certainly not seen or heard when she
discusses anything, whose lips are damp
with spittle spots, mistress of that carefree
yet bankrupt rake from your resort-side camp.

Your town says you are something to behold?
They think your "beauty" matches that of my
Elizabeth? Oh foolish times that mold
dumb men whose tastes can't help but stupefy.

A Multitude of Kisses

Catullus 5

Let's live, Elizabeth, and so let's love,
and let's consider all the rumors of
those prone to talk as worth less than a penny.
The sun can set and rise again, but when we
find that our temporal light has set,
one everlasting night is to be slept.
Give me a thousand kisses, then a hundred,
another thousand, then a second hundred,
still a third thousand, then a hundred more.
Then with so many thousands kept in store,
we'll jumble them around and lose our count
so even we won't know the sure amount,
and then no prying eyes can send ill wishes
because they know the tally of our kisses.

The Problem with Worrying about Being a Prolific Writer

Forgive my trite concerns. A better day
is spent with you instead of at my desk—
a multitude of minutes when we should
have been in bed, in love, conversing while
the sun disturbed our night, or put to use
the picnic basket that we never use,
just one of many idle wedding gifts.
Across the freeway, past the poles and drooping
wires linking telephones, when we had first
moved in to this apartment, months ago,
we noticed the Presidio outside
the window where we put our bed. You asked
me when we'd go and have a picnic there,
and I said then, "Next week," as I have said
for many weeks. Forgive my trite concerns
that sometimes fog my better-willed desires.

Madsong for Elizabeth

Remember when I'd pick you up
in my Buick? We'd cruise the town
       and hit our favorite haunts,
       those bars and restaurants
we'd revel in till they'd close down.

How few were our concerns back then;
you'd work your morning shifts, I'd clean
       and lock the same café
       at night, and we would stay
attached each minute in between.

Oh how we snubbed frugality,
draining our tips on wines that cost
       ten bucks or even more
       down at the corner store
your short-lived street and Broadway crossed.

One roof now—but watch the door tonight;
I'll pick you up to cruise this town,
       like days before this mad
       man wore a tux or had
his mad gal in a wedding gown.

III.

Four Exeter Book Poems (*from the Old English*)

I 'LL DRIVE OUT this song, this journey centered on me,
thoroughly sorrow-ridden. I'm able to say
the miseries I toughed out since I grew up—
the new ones and the old ones—though most are new.
I've always suffered the pain of my exile-paths.
At first my husband left across the lively waves,
away from his countrymen. I was concerned in the night
when I considered the places my prince might be.
Then I was forced to leave there, a friendless outcast,
searching for new service because of my sad need.
My husband's kinsmen, driven by deceit,
devised a plan to split the pair of us
so that we two would live as terribly and as torn apart
as possible within this world. And I did pine.
My husband ordered that I be taken here,
and I've not had a lot of loved or loyal friends
in this or any place. And so my mind is pained
since I found out the man who was my ideal match
was miserable, his mind depressed,
his heart concealed from me, while plotting out his crime.
In carefree conversations we so often claimed
that nothing could divide the two of us
but death alone. Well that has been undone.
These days it's just as though the love
between us never was. Both far and near
I have to suffer the ill will of the one I dearly love.
He told me to stay put among the trees of this forest,
to live beneath this oak, where a cave is hollowed out—
this ancient earth-hall, where I'm worn out with longing.
The valleys are dark, the hills high up,
the shielding hedgerows sharp, all overgrown with briars,
a joyless home. Here my husband's leaving
has often held me cruelly. In other places

lovers are living sweetly. They share a bed
while I walk alone before the daybreak
beneath the oak tree, throughout these earth-holes.
That's where I have to sit each summer-long day.
That's where I'm able to weep for my wretched wanderings,
my load of troubles. And so I just can't ever
cause a break in my mind's cares,
nor in the longing that's kept hold of me in this life.
I hope the young man must always be sad-minded,
his heart's thinking hardened. I hope he has to keep
a cheerful outwardness along with all that worry in his chest,
that mass of constant sorrows. Let the sum of his pleasure
in the world depend on himself alone. And let him be an outlaw
forced to some far-reaching land so that my lover sits
frost-covered by the storm, beneath some stony cliff,
my sad-hearted friend, water flowing around him
in a dreary hall. My dear one is suffering
great sorrows in his mind. He constantly remembers
a much more pleasing home. Misery exists for him
who out of longing has to wait for his beloved.

WELAND saw for himself misery among serpents,
 the stiff-minded noble, stuck out his torments,
had sorrow and longing as his lone companion,
wintercold pain, often came into suffering,
since Nithhad slapped the shackles on him,
tight sinew bonds on the braver man.
  That passed. This can too.

In Beadohild's mind her brothers' death
was not as painful as the plight she faced,
having sensed with certainty
that her belly was growing. She had grim thoughts
when considering how the outcome must be.
  That passed. This can too.

We've heard about what happened to Maethhild,
how the Geat's embraces were bottomless,
how that troubled love took all her sleep away.
  That passed. This can too.

For thirty years Theodoric ruled
the Maerings' city. That was known by many.
  That passed. This can too.

We've learned about the wolfish mind
of Ermanaric. He ruled the people
of the Gothic kingdom. That was a grim king.
Many men sat bound in sorrows,
awaiting hardship, wishing often
that his kingly rule would be overcome.
  That passed. This can too.

The sorrow-filled man sits apart from joys,
darkens in spirit, thinks to himself

that his share of torments must be endless.
He can then consider how common it is
for the wise Lord to change things across this world.
To many men he shows his mercy,
certain splendor, to some a share of hardships.
I'd like to say this thing about myself,
that I was previously the Heodenings' poet,
dear to my lord. Deor was my name.
For many years I had a good position,
a gracious lord, until Heorrenda now,
a song-skilled man, has taken that landright
the nobles' guardian once gifted to me.

    That passed. This can too.

T O MY PEOPLE it's as though a gift was placed before them.
They'll take him if he comes to be conquered.
It's not the same for us.

Wulf's on an island. I'm on another.
His island is secure, encircled by swamp land.
Slaughter-hungry men are there on that island.
They'll take him if he comes to be conquered.
It's not the same for us.

In hopes I traced my Wulf's wandering tracks,
when the weather was rainy and I sat weeping,
when the rough warrior wrapped me in his arms.
I took pleasure in that, yet it was also hateful for me.
Wulf, my Wulf, my hopes for you
have made me sick, your scarce comings,
my anxious mind, not an absence of food.
Are you hearing this, Eadwacer? Our wretched whelp
Wulf carries off to the woods.
One easily breaks apart what was never bound,
the tale of us together.

THIS WALLSTONE is wondrous. Fates have wrecked it.
City sites tumbled. The work of giants crumbles.
Roofs are sunken, towers collapsing,
towers frost-covered and fallen, the frost on the mortar.
Storm tiles are cracked, cut down and caving in,
eaten away by age. The earth's grip holds
the master workers, withered and gone,
the ground's harsh grip, until a hundred generations
of people passed on. Often this wall outstood
kingdom after kingdom, red-stained and lichen-grayed,
persisting beneath storms. Arched and prominent it fell.
Still stands the   piled high.
They broke through
fiercely sharpened
                   shone, the
          skillful creation, old construction
                    stooped from clay coatings.
The mind planned out a clever setup.
The bold-hearted craftsman bound the wall together,
amazingly with wire strips, into ringed structures.
There were bright city buildings, bathhouses in plenty,
a mass of rising archways, the clamor of warriors,
many a meadhall packed with people rejoicing,
until relentless fate reversed all that.

  The slain fell everywhere. Disease days came on.
Death carried off those sword-courageous men.
Their war defenses wasted to desolate spaces.
The cityscape crumbled. Its restorers fell,
its armies into the earth. So now these halls darken,
and the red-curved roof of coiled woodwork
parts from its tiles. This place fell to ruin,
broken to mounds, where many a warrior,
glad-minded and gold-bright, gloriously equipped,
proud and wine-buzzed, once stood in battle gear.

He stared at treasure and silver, at skillfully-made gems,
at prosperity and riches, at precious stones,
at this bright city in its broad kingdom.

    Stone halls stood then. A stream hotly gushed
in a wide surge. A wall surrounded it
in a bright embrace, enclosing the baths,
hot at their heart. That was a handy layout.
Then they let flow
across the gray stone, the hot streams
un-
up to the circular pool. The hot
                    where the baths were.
Then is
                -re. That's a regal thing,
how the   the city

IV.

One Hundred Miles to One More Game of 9-Ball

1.

When in his early twenties, he would drive
from Santa Barbara down to Long Beach and
then back again, each time to find some dive
to meet me in, some place where we would stand
hunched over a pool table, beside red walls
with velvet paintings of calm matadors
or sweaty Elvises. In bigger halls
the gambling tables lined back corridors,

and we would try increasing meager wages.
This pastime, meant to serve as mere distraction
from our weekend studies, yielded stages
that induced vocational attraction.
Soon tournaments ensued, the local matches
that would bring us up to San Francisco
(his trips habitual, mine in rare batches)
or take us home, back down to San Diego.

2.

Almost a decade later now he spends
most noons to sevens at Society.
Slamming into each break, he comprehends
the spread and every possibility
for running out the 1 through 9. At night
he cooks calzones and pizzas at the shop
he worked at in our high-school years, the slight
and narrow storefront where I'd help him mop

to earn a quick five bucks. These days I take
my cue out of its case on rare occasions
and seldom set more than a drink at stake;
my stroke is rusty from new aspirations.
Nine credits shy of getting his B.A.,
he lets the mounting years extend the reach
of that expected goal, turning away
the safer paths he hears most others preach.

He is by no means limited in choices
for the daunting years, and he's aware
of that regressive attitude of voices
that speak success. At present they declare
that he is wasting both his mind and time,
but if one day he's seen on television,
competing for some prize, then all will chime
how they had known he'd made the right decision.

Bird Watching at the Coast of La Jolla

for N. A., per jocum

The landscape can't be beat. The coastline boasts
the most attractive beaches in the west,
the waves I grew up in, by cliffs where hosts
of pelicans and cormorants seek rest,
clustered under crags while bellies digest

plucked fish. The most voracious avis stays
affixed in plainer sight where it pursues.
The coast is overrun with popinjays
who perch and brood in nests with ocean views,
all feathered by their BMWs.

Words Outside

Glimpsing an old *Times* on the balcony,
I noticed that a web had been set up
among the lower leaves and loose debris

that circumvent our calathea's pot.
The web had snatched some type of smaller fly
whose body, though dead still, had yet to rot.

And then I saw the deathtrap's architect
slide down a sturdy thread to greet his prize,
the weaver whose skilled efforts I have wrecked

whenever he has built near where I sit.
This time I let his web remain intact
and watched as he sucked down each liquid bit.

I realized that I had never seen
this done before and that so many things
I've learned from books and speech and life's routine

I claim by sight, when really they've been taught.
And if I knew the sum, I'd marvel at
the things I think I've seen that I have not.

Lines

Here's what we'll do
because this card is crammed and that one boasts
          a one-time deal
for moving debts onto a lower rate.

Because that card is crammed and this one boasts
          a bit of space
from moving debts onto a lower rate,
          this one maintains

          a bit of space
for this week's groceries and last month's heat.
          That one maintains
a back-up stratagem that we could use

for next week's groceries and this month's heat.
          On that one there,
a backed-up stratagem. That we could use
          an increased line

          on this one here
is no surprise, but that one offered us
          an increased line
to make sure we can pay. Each coming month

is no surprise. But this one offered us
          a one-time deal
to make sure we can pay each coming month.
          Here's what we'll do:

Eighteen Wheels

The billboards pointing out the porno shops
      that dot this stretch of 70
         are placed conveniently
a mile or so before the service stops.
It's clear where one can pull aside and enter
      Passions or The Lion's Den,
         especially in winter,
when the roadside scenery is pretty
desolate on route to Kansas City

or St. Louis. Most frequenters are haulers
of the goods embodying earned dollars,
      the men whose work confines
     them to a cab for every shift.
False hope embeds itself in vibrant signs,
a lift of heart to stave off loneliness,
      a whisper or a cry
     reminding weary passersby
that life is not comprised of only this.

On Winter Beards and the Length of Seasons

Lines Written after a Frigid Midwest March

With April on its way, I shaved,
and I was only slightly shocked
to see a double chin emerge.
Three months, I thought. Three months of weights
will sharpen it again. Three months
will thicken up the arms and pecs.

A season's length is adequate
for self improvements, whether they
are realized or brushed aside.

It measures expectations in
a manageable dose. It fuels
the hope that what waits just ahead
will not resemble this. And then
it fools us with a different scene
so we think all is not the same.

First Spring in Columbia, Missouri

Catullus 46

At last the spring revives more pleasing weather.
At last the clamor of the dismal sky
is calmed by the delightful winds of Zephyr.

Before too long a sultry surge will roast
this Midwest town. Let's go somewhere. Let's tour
these plains, then jet to California's coast.

At last my mind is stirred, at last inspired,
craving to wander in this warmth and coolness.
At last my feet awaken with desire.

Take care, dear friends, all you who first set out
from home on well-mapped paths but now return
by roads that form an unexpected route.

To an Acquaintance on a Tragic Occasion

Catullus 96

If any sweet or beneficial thing
    can go where silent graves remain,
    Alfred, from our grievous pain,
the longing that enables us to bring
    old loves to life and makes us weep
    for friendships we no longer keep,
surely Anita's thoughts are not of grief
    for her too early death, but of
    the joy she feels from your great love.

New Year's Eve in Denver

On Jan. 1, 2007, in the earliest hours of the morning,
Darrent Williams, a cornerback for the Denver Broncos,
was murdered in downtown Denver just hours after
the team lost the season-ending game the night before.

On New Year's Eve I toured the downtown streets
of Denver with my in-laws and my wife.
       The wintry air gave life
to bundled limbs and feet that trampled snow,
and we recalled the blessings and defeats
we'd met that year, the things that never show
       on credit-card receipts
nor catalog the depths of stuff we know.

At night we walked down 16th Street, then ate
at Palominos, where we saw the pour
       of fireworks before
returning to the Queen Anne B&B.
At some point in the night—when not yet late—
a Hummer limousine passed by, and we
       supposed some eager date
was happy to ignore frugality.

But over coffee in the early hours
the morning news declared that you'd been killed;
       a host of bullets spilled
into the side of that same limousine.
I knew of you and your athletic powers,
and we, each fostering a different dream,
       assumed that time devours
most lives with age and not the unforeseen.

Two months have passed and there's no resolution

to declare. In California few
           are still aware of you
and what transpired just as this year began.
But I remember you and the confusion
of those morning hours, when every plan
           you'd made met its conclusion—
by some false friend or some disgruntled fan.

Lines from a Former Chaplain's Assistant
at North County Jail in Oakland, California

Eleven years ago they moved him from
North County to San Quentin. I thought of him
this morning for the first time in some years
and wished that I'd been pained at my indifference.
Eleven years ago we prayed together,
clasping our hands inside an empty room—
the two of us, two chairs, and nothing else
behind a steel door and two-inch glass.

Two deputies would bring him out in chains
and I'd be locked alone inside that room,
awaiting their arrival. They'd shuffle in,
a linked trio of gray and red and gray,
and then I'd ask them to unlock his hands.
I was 18 and 19 then, between
the end of high school and the start of college.
I masked my youth behind an unkempt beard
and spent off-hours lifting heavy weights.

His transfer to Death Row occurred in May,
or maybe June, and I'd head out a few
months later too, back down to San Diego.

He and the other inmates wrote me letters
after that. I spent a year or so
responding, and some of them kept writing me
long after I'd stopped sending them replies.
I don't remember when I lost the drive
to be a prison chaplain, whether it was
a made decision or a loss of interest.

I thought of him this morning, whether he is
among the living, whether my former self
is present even with inactive hands.

V.

A Charm for Unfruitful Land

from the Old English

Here is the remedy for curing your fields if they refuse to grow well, or any place that has been improperly acted upon by sorcery or witchcraft:

In the night, before the day breaks, remove four turfs from the four corners of the land, and mark how they stood before. Then take oil and honey and yeast, and milk from each of the cattle on the land, and a piece from every type of tree growing in the land, except for hard trees, and a piece of every well-known herb, except for buckbean, and then add holy water to it all, and then drip it three times on the underside of the turfs, and then say these words: *Crescite*, grow, *et multiplicamini*, and multiply, *et replete*, and fill up, *terre*, the earth; *in nomine patris et filii et spiritus sancti sit benedicti*. And say the *Pater noster* as often as the other. And afterward carry the turfs to the church, and have the masspriest sing four masses over the turfs, and turn the green sides toward the altar, and after that bring the turfs back to where they originally were before the sun sets. And out of juniper wood make four signs of Christ for them, and on each end write, *Matheus* and *Marcus*, *Lucas* and *Iohannes*. Lay one sign of Christ in each corner's pit. Then say, *Crux Matheus, crux Marcus, crux Lucas, crux sanctus Iohannes*. Then take the turfs and set them on top of the signs, and then say these words nine times: *Crescite . . .* and the *Pater noster* as often. And then turn yourself eastward, and bow humbly nine times, and then say these words:

> I stand facing east. I pray for favors.
> I pray to the famous Lord, pray to the great Prince.
> I pray to the holy Keeper of heaven's kingdom.
> I pray to the earth and the heaven above
> and the celebrated Saint Mary
> and heaven's power and the high hall
> that with the Lord's grace I might let loose this spell—
> reveal it through my teeth, with a resolved mind—
> to wake these plants for our worldly use,
> to fill these lands, because of firm belief,
> to beautify this plain's turfs, exactly as the prophet said,
> that he who might deal out his alms commendably
> would have help in the earthly kingdom, through kindness of
> the Lord.

Then turn yourself around three times, moving with the sun. Then stretch out flat on the ground and count out the litanies there, and then say, *Sanctus, sanctus, sanctus,* up to its end. Then with outstretched arms sing the *Benedicite* and the *Magnificat* and the *Pater noster* three times, and offer it to Christ and to Saint Mary and to the holy cross as a praise and as an honor, and as a glory to the one who possesses the land and to all those who are subjugated to him. When all of that has been accomplished, go get unfamiliar seed from almsmen, taking twice as much as one normally would, and gather together all the plowing tools. Then in the wood cut a hole for incense and fennel and hallowed soap and hallowed salt. Then take the seed, set it on the plow's body, and say:

> Erce, Erce, Erce—earth's mother—
> may the Leader of all—the everlasting Lord—
> grant you fields that grow and flourish,
> that are enlarged and made lively,
> tall shafts, shining crops,
> and the broad barley-crops,
> and the white wheat-crops,
> and every one of the earth's crops.
> May the everlasting Lord
> and his holy saints in the heavens
> allow the plowing to be protected against all enemies,
> to be preserved against all possible threats,
> those sorceries sown widely through the land.
> I pray to the Ruler now, to him who wrought the world,
> that there would not be a woman so eloquent nor a man so
> cunning
> who could upset the speech just spoken.

Then drive the plow forward and open up the first furrow. Then say:

> Soil, be healthy!—mother of humankind.
> Be growing in God's embrace,
> filled up with food as a benefit to people.

Then take flour of every kind, and bake a loaf of bread the width of cupped hands, and knead it with milk and with holy water, and place it beneath the first furrow. Then say:

Field full of food for humankind—
bright-blooming—be blessed
because of the holy name of him who shaped the heaven,
as well as the earth on which we live.
May the God who formed the plains grant us increasing grace
so that each grain might come to be a gain for us.

Then say, *Crescite . . . In nomine patris . . . sit benedicti* three times, and *Amen*
and the *Pater noster* three times as well.

VI.

Rubliw for Tom Waits

Hey Waits,
Keep loose the gates
and flood this land with crates
of tunes that pipe our candid states.
Your blend of word and melody creates
a sweet and sordid joy that skates
across our dirtied slates.
Each age awaits
such greats.

A Too-late Letter to Thom Gunn

T. G. (1929-2004)

Dear Mr. Gunn,

      You've helped me loosen up.
I used to think that syllables combined
to form some thing in likeness to a cup,
some holder that was rigidly defined.
Instead, you've demonstrated that a poem
in structured verse is not composed of clay,
nor is it chipped and fashioned from a stone,
revealing patterns from what's cut away.
The likeness of a cadenced poem reflects
the composition of musicians' notes;
unbruised, unbent, each well-placed word collects
within a frame of ink that somehow floats.
Your lines succeed because they clearly show
that verse is not a chopped up paragraph
in which words run without a pleasant flow.

                    Indebted to you,
                    Derek Updegraff

To Gerry Locklin, Professor Emeritus

on his retirement from over four decades of teaching

I've read that most of Schubert's works remained
unknown in his brief life, that decades passed
before a symphony or opera gained
a portion of the praises now amassed.

This is the case with many artists who
don't get to realize the impacts made
by their results, the efforts that pass through
each generation with their worth reweighed.

But this is not the case with you, who's seen
his many printed poems and fictions clutched
by eager hands, and what is less routine
and what can never be assessed or touched

remains imprinted on your students' minds,
an admiration that securely binds.

A Proverb from Winfrid's Time

from the Old English

The sluggard is often slow in making choices—
dismissing tough pursuits, then dying alone for that.

Horace to Leuconoë

Horace, Odes 1.11

Don't ask, sharp-minded girl, tonight's dear friend,
exactly how much time we have to spend
until we meet our ends. If one possessed
that fact, it'd be a sin, so don't you test
predictions, even the most-tempting ones.
It's better to endure whatever comes,
whether fortune decided on more winters
or if these minutes mark the final winter
we'll be dealt, this last dire season that
wears down the seas outside as they combat
opposing rocks. Use common sense, and take
the dregs out of the wine, and now forsake
the hopes a year can't bring about. As we
discuss these things, the jealous seconds flee:
enjoy this night, the ripeness we possess,
relying on tomorrow much, much less.

I Hate and Love My Girl

Catullus 85

I hate and love my girl. Perhaps
you question how I can relapse

from adoration to disgust
so easily. Ask if you must,

but I have no idea. In fact
I seldom choose how I'll react

to her. I feel it done to me,
and I am left in agony.

Ostentatious Liqueurs

Horace, Odes 1.38

I hate ornate and showy drinks, Stephen.
The cocktails mixed with vivid colors cause
me grief. Don't search the fridge for fruit, even
for that final bottle of grenadine,
    and please put down those stupid straws
        of purple, orange, and green.

I'm worried that your fussy self has no
desire to drink a simple beer from time
to time. A beer is not unfit, you know,
for such as you, whether or not it's made
    abroad, nor me, apt to recline
        and drink beneath the shade.

Catullus to Varus, Regarding a Mutual Friend

Catullus 22

That Suffenus, a guest in both our homes,
is charming, full of wit, and quite urbane,
and he produces piles and piles of poems.

I think he's written thousands, maybe more,
but unlike us, he doesn't jot them on
recycled paper or scratch bits before

the lines are set. He writes on nothing less
than sheets of cotton, watermarked, then binds
the bunch in vellum at some self-serve press.

Our shrewd Suffenus, when his poems are read,
relinquishes his charms and seems more like
some ditch digger, or goat milker, instead

of his deft self. How can this be? Our friend
who was a dear and clever man becomes
inept right when his awful poems are penned,

and he is never more elated than
when writing poems, delighting in himself
so much. We're all deceived now and again

like him, for every one of us is known
as a Suffenus, entitled to delusions,
but others' faults obstruct us from our own.

Horace to Postumus, Regarding a Somber Truth

Horace, Odes 2.14

This course is rough, my friend, my long and valued friend.
The years dart by, and no degree of honest living
    can lessen wrinkles, make age more forgiving,
        or force unyielding death to bend.

There is no gift so large or fine, though some have tried
to give one, that quiets tearless Pluto, who's imprisoned
    triple-bodied Geryon and lust-driven
        Tityus, without a fight, beside

the dreadful current. That water must be sailed across
by all, each one of us relying on the earth
    for sustenance, if we're of noble birth
        or farmers of those very crops.

With pointless caution we'll avoid the violent ocean
and pounding waves, or any conflict too severe.
    When winter's hostile weather hits, we'll fear
        the cold with bodily devotion.

Cocytos must be seen by all who lived above
it, as must the other black and sluggish rivers,
    along with Danaus' daughters, bridegroom killers,
        and Sisyphus condemned to shove

his boulder. Your house must be abandoned with your land,
and certainly your pleasing wife, and all of these
    magnificent and labored-over trees
        you cultivate by your own hand.

Your smarter heir won't pause to drink your vintage labels,
the wine you guarded with a hundred keys. He'll stain
    the pavement with what's harder to obtain
        than that poured out at royal tables.

Arma Virumque Cano

I've tried in vain to write about these months,
to focus on the sickness, not the man
admired by multitudes of students once
committed to his class, the dad I plan
on mimicking one day, whose love outran
frustration with the greatest ease, and not
the husband whose sincere devotion taught

me how a man is meant to treat his bride.
The winter hours were harsh, but spring has come
and cleared away the tubes that lay beside
your bed. Those icy streams descending from
the bags of medicine at last succumb
to your resilience, your desire not to
allow the cancer to impede all you

still have to do and witness in your life:
to walk your only daughter down the aisle,
to celebrate five decades with your wife,
to see the first of your grandchildren smile
as you embrace her in your arms awhile,
as God will hold you once your time has set,
but that appointment is not yet, not yet.

The spring has come at last. The grass returns
to quiet fields, the leaves enclose the trees,
and just as every budding leaflet yearns
to hold its grip, your body wants to seize
the strength it once produced in great degrees.
With colored cheeks you'll soon regain the hair
on surfaces where winter left you bare,

and this new season will outlast mere days
and will remain for many, many years.
A storm should not be why a son conveys
unsaid esteem or why a father hears
the full extent of how his son reveres
his dad, whom he desired to imitate
when he was young but longs to emulate

now that he has progressed in sense and age.
Your too rare combination of regard
and erudition lets your words engage
your class, which learns about much more than hard
yet pleasing verse. Your students don't discard
the Virgil or the dignity they learn,
and now they wait and pray for your return.

The Edge Where Atlas Stands

A routine blood test with my dad's oncologist
   brought me inside another waiting room.
   As resolute as any to resist
   the storm, my dad—though he is not immune
     to everything as we
    when young once thought our parents were—
fought through immeasurable hours to endure
    his chemotherapy.

Across from where I sat, a mother and her son
   were talking as I read a magazine.
   It looked as though each loved the other one;
   while speaking, they kept little space between
    their laughter and their smiles.
   Though his condition was severe,
she managed to conceal a parent's greatest fear
    as he went through his trials.

His forearm veins now freshly stuck, my dad returned.
   (They'd taken out the catheter that passed
   from chest to world and let so freely.) We learned
   his white-cell count was on the rise at last,
    but they could not yet tell
    the damage of the storm until
more tests and time progressed. I pray the waves keep still
    and never, never swell.

Our choices are our own, but things are set so none
can choose another body's burdens or its strains:
a mother can't switch places with her stricken son;
a healthy son can't shoulder all his father's pains.

Postbellum

on my dad's return to the classroom

It seems as if mere days have passed
since I was sitting in your chair.
    A sly imposter masked
by your same chin, decked in a suit
and tie and shirt like you would wear,
    I was the substitute

who'd come to hear your students give
the recitations they'd prepared.
    I'd listen and relive
my high-school days as each would go,
seeing myself, awkward and scared,
    reciting Cicero.

But you have managed to reclaim
the role that no one else could fill,
    and you, who overcame
such cruel adversity, surpassed
my comprehension of a will.
    Now I, appearing cast

from some similar mold, remain
amazed by strength and faith displayed
    despite your length of pain.
Know this: no orator of any year
could tell of all the impacts made
    by having you still here.

VII.

Elizabeth Standing before Our Bedroom Mirror

She stands before the mirror and lifts her shirt,
exhibiting her stomach's even skin
    but not what grows within.
  She asks me if she's showing yet.
"Not yet," I say. She looks a little hurt,
as if these early weeks of knowing should

reveal themselves in more than just our faces.
They say that it's the size of a blueberry
    now, that it is barely
  there at all. But its heart beats,
and she's the one in tune with how its space is
subtly getting larger. I pull the sheets

aside and crawl in bed, but she remains
before the mirror, inspecting every view,
    guiding her palm into
  an O that wanes at each rotation.
"You're wrong," she says. "She's here." Her fingers frame
an inch of skin revealing her location.

Walking around Our Neighborhood, Midway through the First Trimester

She says she's terrified to have a daughter,
that she would screw her up somehow, infuse
the same mentality that often brought her
to starvation, the point when she would choose

the slimmest version of a ballerina's
body. Now as a teacher she recalls
how difficult each later teenage year was,
and so she can console each girl who falls

headlong into a similar position.
I say her worry just might reconcile
this fear, that when we whisper some admission
of terror we'll work to shield her from that trial,

and we're both fit to guide our kids around
the baggage that we've dragged across the ground.

Assurance

At four months in she hasn't felt a kick.
This worries her, but I insist it's normal.
She knows far more than I but likes to hear
me say, "It's normal." Each week she lets me know
what elements are being defined. Last week
the fingerprints began to pattern; and now
the taste buds grow acute, and it can slide
its tongue out of its cheerio-sized mouth.
She's thinking it's a boy because she craves
more meat than usual. I shrug and say
how I could picture both my son or daughter
demanding that she eat a steak for dinner.

She's worried that she hasn't felt a kick.
Her friend suggested that she drink a glass
of juice and lie completely still. She's in
the kitchen now, alone, stirring some type
of fruit juice with our longest wooden spoon.
Tonight there will be tears of one kind or
another; but first she'll drink her glass, walk down
the hall, and climb atop our bed, stretched out
with hands positioned on her budding skin,
awaiting the first flutter, the only one's
assurance that can keep her mind from worry.

First Purchase after the Sonogram

We called you "darling" months before we glimpsed
    your image on the monitor
    and claimed the pronouns "she" and "her"
for you alone, and there, pressed up against

your mother's skin, you were drawn out in sound:
    your limbs and digits, ribs and spine,
    assembling in a new design
of "she" and "darling," every movement bound

by photograph as our technician paused it,
    offering us each ashen still,
    the varied angles that will fill
the little onesie dangling in your closet.

A Country Road and Other Roads

Wouldn't it, Didi, be really too bad? (Pause.)
When you think of the beauty of the way. (Pause.)
And the goodness of the wayfarers.

Samuel Beckett, *Waiting for Godot*

The path is lovely. As lovely as this two o'clock
    cluster at the local Steak 'n Shake—
    this trio seated at a two-top:
      a child not quite awake
placed evenly between her father and her mother,
    each one still sweet on the other,
    out dining for his thirtieth
      on a permissive Thursday.

The path is lovely, dear one. Lovely but difficult.
For you I pray adversity in measured doses,
    that we might have the means to petal
      your path in stony places—
      and strength to let it settle
      without us, where it flowers
    because of goodness from some other farers.

Same Song Remixed

Place me in unfertile fields where no
tree is revived by a summer breeze . . .

I will love Lalage, sweetly laughing,
sweetly talking.

Horace, *Odes I.22*

He was a lousy bouncer back in Long Beach.
The pay was good, in cash and under
the table. But there are things that one assumes
about a man who's 6-foot-4 and weighs
225, who's got a crooked nose
and makes his way by handling the riffraff.

The bar was down on 7th Street. He had
to quit that gig before some meddler tried
to make a name off him. A few blocks west
and south of there, the Goth kids lined outside
the Art Theatre on Saturdays to watch
The Rocky Horror Picture Show again.

The port town kids of his childhood admired
the weathered sailors. The ink from their tattoos
had wandered out of line and turned their arms
to murky casings showing worn mementos.
The kids would see them by the piers and bait shops,
imagining their own arms decked with smudges.

The other day he drank with an old timer
there in Missouri who said that fatherhood
would soften him, that years of changing diapers
deprives men of *machismo.* His word, he marked
the air with it, carved out a spot above
the youngster's jacket freshly stained with spit-up.

Our hero there will be all right. I watched
him hale the cab, then kiss his sleeping daughter.
Place him in stony fields devoid of shade
and summer breezes. Place him in waters
oppressed by violent skies. You'll find him there
unscathed—sweetly laughing, sweetly talking.

Lullaby

My voice is coarse from singing "Twinkle Twinkle."
We rock within the glow beside her crib,
clutching each other halfway through my watch.
"Again," she says. "Again, Twinkle Twinkle."
I'd sung a string of others hours ago,
but there's no moving past these six lines now.
I sing. She quiets. Then as the final
syllable is falling, she squeaks, "Again."
She doesn't mind my raspy voice, likes it
even, and I like being unashamed
of it, how I sometimes manage in the pews.
Our loop replays. Her echo slips. I reach
the second "How I wonder what you are,"
and she allows the line to close, inserting
punctuation with her silence. I stand,
cradle her down, then slide my arms out,
but I've not let our song come to a rest,
repeating in my head the final words,
you are, you are, you are, collecting open
clauses needing her to reach completion.

At Nineteen Months, in the Half-light of Early September

My daughter wakes me with a finger, pressing
me to raise my lids. I do, and then
we take each other in. Her mom's caressing
her slight body, placed between us when
she cried out at the lauding hour, awaiting
consolation. She says, "A bunny rabbit"
as she pats my arm, anticipating
my correction. I cultivate her habit.
"Ground hog," I say, and pat the same tattoo.
"No," she says. "No. A bunny rabbit," showing
me the image one more time. I view
my arm inquiringly. Her face is glowing.
"Okay," I say. "A bunny rabbit." Her lesson's
done, awakening my day's confessions.

Loop

He's in the living room, alone
for now, his wife unwinding in the shower
                at the hour
        when the evening Autumn gray has gone,
                their daughter curling up
in her footed onesie.

                        The room is still,
but in this rest Vivaldi's violins
                are whirling up
                the violent winds
that leave the scattered drawings on the floor
        unmoved. He sits surrounded by them.
        His wife had drawn some type of flower.
                "A daffodil,"
                their daughter told them.
He'd drawn his childhood fish. She'd pointed to it,
                "Orange fish."
"That's right," he'd said. And then, "A garibaldi."
They'd colored in the Spring time of Vivaldi.
        She grabbed a different orange than his,
                then left her other images
to crayon a different splotch, whispering to it,
                "A garibaldi."

He sits there still. A Winter track begins
                to skip. The violins
become corralled within an O of seconds,
                attempting to break through it
                with their violence.

He lets the skipping loop, not attending
        to the freeze, but attending
to the slowness of the shower's water,
imagining the imprint of their daughter
        fresh on his wife's arms,
imagining the movement of her arms,
    the caressing of their daughter
        when she sang to her,
    the caressing of her own skin now,
now as she soaps her budding skin, the water
        thickening,
                then running,
    now as she stands before the mirror,
        frontways,
                    then sideways,
    gliding her hands along the space
    preparing to grow again, again
to grow, while he is sitting in his place,
            there,
        awaiting her,
        awaiting them.

Notes

The editions I used for the Old English and Latin translations were *The Exeter Book*, edited by George Philip Krapp and Elliott Van Kirk Dobbie (Columbia University Press, 1936); *The Anglo-Saxon Minor Poems*, edited by Elliott Van Kirk Dobbie (Columbia University Press, 1942); *The Old English Elegies: A Critical Edition and Genre Study*, by Anne L. Klinck (McGill-Queen's University Press, 1992); *The Exeter Anthology of Old English Poetry*, edited by Bernard J. Muir, 2 volumes, revised 2nd edition (University of Exeter Press, 2000); and *Catullus and Horace: Selections from Their Lyric Poetry*, edited by Andrew C. Aronson and Robert Boughner (Longman, 1988).

"A Charm for Unfruitful Land": This Anglo-Saxon charm survives in a tenth-century manuscript. Similar to other extant charms of the period, the text is a mixture of prose and verse. As was customary with the copying of all Old English poetry, the verse lines are not lineated in the manuscript but appear written across the page in the same manner as prose. Following common editorial practice, I draw attention to the verse sections through lineation.

Four Exeter Book Poems: The Old English poems in the tenth-century codex known as The Exeter Book do not have author-given titles. It is usually clear when one poem ends and another begins because the scribe leaves space between the works and starts each new poem with a large decorative letter. The practice of titling was not an aspect of Old English poetics. The editorial titles these four poems are generally known by are "The Wife's Lament," "Deor," "Wulf and Eadwacer," and "The Ruin." The section of the manuscript containing "The Ruin" is damaged, causing some lines to be incomplete. To learn more about the manuscript lives of Old English poems and the translation process, see Derek Updegraff, "The Translatability of Manuscript Pages Containing Old English Verse (with an Illustrative Translation of *The Exeter Book*, Folios 98r-101r and 124r-124v)," *Texas Studies in Literature and Language* 56.1 (2014): 1-41.

Acknowledgments

I'd like to thank the editors of the following journals, in which many of these poems and translations first appeared, sometimes in slightly different form:

Bellowing Ark, Cave Region Review, The Chiron Review, Christianity & Literature, The Classical Outlook: Journal of the American Classical League, Ezra: An Online Journal of Translation, Front Range Review, Lucid Rhythms, The Lyric, The Maine Review, Measure: A Review of Metrical Poetry, Natural Bridge, The New Formalist, Over the Transom, The Pennsylvania Review, The Raintown Review, Re)verb, The Rotary Dial, Saint Katherine Review, THINK: A Journal of Poetry, Criticism, and Reviews, and *Windhover.*

Some poems also appeared in these anthologies: *Beside the City of Angels: An Anthology of Long Beach Poetry* (World Parade Books, 2010) and *Because I Said So: Poems on the Happiness and Crappiness of Parenthood* (Aortic Books, 2011); and some poems appeared in these limited-edition chapbooks: *Between Pit Stops at Late-night Diners* (dOOm-AH Books, 2008), *The Edge Where Atlas Stands* (dOOm-AH Books, 2008), and *Twenty Gently Used & Pre-owned Poems* (The New Formalist Press, 2012).

I'd also like to thank Scott Cairns, Aliki Barnstone, Gerald Locklin, Charles Harper Webb, Julie Sophia Paegle, Melissa Range, Johanna Kramer, Britt Mize, Anne L. Klinck, Peter Ramey, John A. Nieves, Julie Christenson, Noé Ruvalcaba, Jennifer Tronti, David Middleton, Timothy Steele, and Kimberly Verhines at SFA Press.

Most of all I'd like to thank my wife, Elizabeth, to whom this book is dedicated, our daughters, my parents, my sister, and the rest of my family and friends for being constant sources of encouragement and companionship.

Derek Updegraff has published poems, translations, and short stories in *The Carolina Quarterly*, *The Classical Outlook*, *CutBank*, *The Greensboro Review*, *Metamorphoses*, *the minnesota review*, *North Dakota Quarterly*, *The Southampton Review*, *Tikkun*, and other journals. His essays have appeared in *Oral Tradition*, *Pacific Coast Philology*, and *Texas Studies in Literature and Language*, and he is a contributing writer for *The Encyclopedia of Medieval Literature in Britain* (Wiley-Blackwell, 2017). His debut fiction collection, *The Butcher's Tale and Other Stories* (2016), is also available from Stephen F. Austin State University Press. He grew up in San Diego and earned an M.F.A. in creative writing from California State University, Long Beach, and a Ph.D. in English from the University of Missouri. He currently lives in Riverside, California, and teaches at Azusa Pacific University.

CPSIA information can be obtained
at www.ICGtesting.com
Printed in the USA
FFHW021831201118
49517726-53878FF